GW00360030

IS IT TRUE?
Evidence
for the Bible

Clive Anderson and Brian Edwards

CPR DayOne

About this booklet

The Bible is full of people, places and events that are set in real points of history. So you can check it out and discover just how reliable it is.

The Christian Bible is a thrilling account of God's plan for the human race from the beginning of creation to the end of the world and beyond. Each book within the Bible follows a carefully ordered plan building towards the complete picture. That picture is God's rescue plan for the human race through Jesus Christ.

Too often people dismiss the Bible as unreliable without realising that archaeologists have uncovered so many things that confirm its accuracy.

What follows in this booklet are just a few examples of the evidence demonstrating that the Bible is a book of accurate and reliable history.

This is only a 'taster' of the much larger and fully referenced book *Evidence for the Bible*. For details of this see inside the back cover.

Many even small and seemingly insignificant discoveries point to the reality of people whose stories are told in the Bible.

Here are two clay seal impressions of two kings of Judah. It is hard to doubt their existence when we have their ID cards!

*A seal impression inscribed with the words:
'Belonging to Ahaz [son of] Yehotam [Jotham], king of
Judah' — precisely as we read in 2 Kings 16:1.*

*This is the seal impression
'Belonging to Hezekiah (son of) Ahaz, king of Judah'.*

1. Noah and the world-wide flood

Stories of a global flood are found in the traditions of nations across the world, including Iran, Egypt, Russia, China, India, Mexico, Peru and Hawaii.

It is common for people to dismiss the Bible's account of Noah and the great flood as nothing more than legend – a made up story. However, the folklore of many cultures has preserved the record of something cataclysmic that happened very early in human history.

Some researchers have found almost 270 stories of a flood that destroyed the whole of civilization. In fact these come from every continent except Antarctica! The details are often bizarre and very different from the sane account in Genesis chapters 6 to 9, but they have in common a great flood that destroyed everything except animals and a few people who escaped.

Of these many accounts, Christians believe that the biblical account is the true record given by God to Moses. The details are reasonable and the exact dimensions of the Ark are given in the Bible. Naval architects have shown that an ark built to these dimensions was well able to ride out a global flood for a long period of time.

Jesus certainly accepted the story as a historical fact (see Matthew 24:37–39).

The Gilgamesh epic is one of the best known accounts of a global flood from the ancient world and closest to the record in the Bible. Gilgamesh is searching for immortality. He meets Ut-napishti who tells how he found immortality by surviving a world-wide flood. Ut-napishti was instructed by the god Ea to build a great boat and bring his family and representatives of all living creatures into it. Details of the construction were given to him, and the great six-decker survived the flood that destroyed the rest of mankind. Apparently even the gods were frightened by the deluge! After a week, 'the sea grew quiet, the tempest was still, the flood ceased' and Ut-napishti sent out a dove, a swallow and a raven – the raven did not return. Ut-napishti left the boat and offered sacrifices to the gods. As a reward Ut-napishti and his wife were given immortality.

The clay tablet describing the Gilgamesh epic is dated around 650 BC but is thought to be a copy of one much older. This was found in the ruins of the library of the last great king of Assyria in Nineveh and is now in the British Museum in London.

2. Who were the Hittites?

For a long time some scholars doubted whether a people called the Hittites ever existed because the only known reference to them was in the Bible.

The Hittites are often mentioned in the first book of the Bible, Genesis. For example Genesis 10:15; 15:20; 23:3. According to the Bible they were a powerful and feared people as is evident from 1 Kings 10:29 and 2 Kings 7:6. One of king David's military officers was a Hittite (2 Samuel 11:6-7).

In 1906 their ancient capital of Hattusas (Boğhazköy in Turkey) was uncovered and they are now known to have been a very enlightened and educated people. The Hittite empire was founded around 1700 BC, and from 1400 they became one of the great powers in diplomatic and trade contact with other kings. Pharaoh Ramesses II of Egypt knew them by the name 'Kheta' and in his great temple at Abu Simbel he celebrated with pictures of the battle against them at Kadesh in 1274 BC.

By 1200 BC Hittite power was broken and their empire declined.

Today, no one questions the existence of the Hittites.

Hittite prisoners depicted on Ramesses' victory temple at Abu Simbel, Egypt. Although the pharaoh presented this as a great victory, the battle of Kadesh was a costly stalemate that eventually led to a peace treaty.

3. The earliest reference to Israel

The fact that the descendants of Abraham, known as the people of Israel, occupied Canaan from an early date is now accepted by many leading authorities.

On this black granite Stela is an inscription from Merneptah who was the Pharaoh of Egypt from 1213 to 1203 BC. Merneptah boasts of his personal achievements and victories and it concludes with a short list of cities and people in Canaan defeated by the king. It includes the phrase 'Israel is laid waste and his seed is not.' Merneptah exaggerates in the suggestion that Israel has been annihilated.

Egyptologists agree that of the eight names on the stela, seven refer to a land whilst the reference to Israel refers to a people group, indicating that at this time Israel was not yet settled in a land it could call its own.

The Merneptah Stela reveals that by 1209 BC the Egyptians knew the Israelites as a well organized people group who were well established in Canaan—what is now known as Israel—but not yet in full control of their territory.

This fits the period of the Judges when the Israelites were settling in Canaan and Yahweh allowed their enemies to oppress them from 1356 to 1050 BC.

This granite inscription from the reign of Pharaoh Merneptah in 1209 BC is in the Cairo Museum. At present it is the earliest reference to the people of Israel outside the Bible.

4. King David, a legendary hero?

David, king of Israel, is a central figure in the Bible with fifty-nine chapters describing his life and reign and many psalms recorded as his.

David lived around one thousand years before Jesus was born. In spite of his importance there was no evidence of him outside the Bible. This led many scholars to assume he never existed. They suggested that David was merely a legendary hero invented by scribes to keep up the morale of Jewish exiles in Persia five hundred years before Jesus was born.

An inscription found at Tel Dan in Northern Israel in 1993, comes from the time of king Hazael of Syria around 790 BC. The king boasts that he killed the king of Israel and 'the king of *Bayt-Dawid*'. That last phrase means either the 'house (dynasty) of David' or the 'city of David'. Either way, it is a clear reference to king David and only 200 years after

The Tel Dan inscription provides clear evidence that the 'house of David' was known less than two hundred years after his death.

his death. That is 250 years before the so-called 'legend' of David was made up!

Professor Kenneth Kitchen, a leading archaeologist at Liverpool University, comments, 'It cannot seriously be interpreted in any other way'.

The Tel Dan inscription places the existence of David beyond any reasonable doubt. As one scholar wrote: 'There was a David. He was a king. And he founded a dynasty.'

But there's more evidence for David. On the Mesha Stela (sometimes called the Moabite Stone) the king of Moab boasts of his defeat of Israel and refers to 'the house (dynasty) of David'. Most archaeologists accept this. You can read about the king of Moab in 2 Kings 3. The Mesha Stela is dated around 840 BC—that's only 120 years after king David.

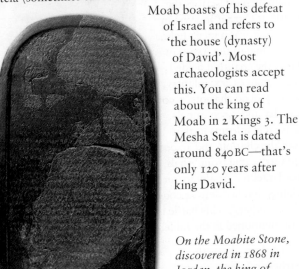

On the Moabite Stone, discovered in 1868 in Jordan, the king of Moab refers to 'the house of David'.

5. 'A strong man, unsparing'

This is how Shalmaneser III, the king of Assyria, boasted about himself. And two kings of Israel had reason to be afraid.

Ahab of Israel joined a coalition of twelve kings to oppose Shalmaneser. On a limestone stela to honour himself and his gods, Shalmaneser describes the battle at Qarqar in Syria in 853 BC. It was a mega fight. According to the Assyrian king, the coalition fielded more than 61,000 infantry, almost 4,000 chariots, 1,900 cavalry and 1,000 camels. The stela informs us that half the chariots and 10,000 infantry came from 'Ahab, the Israelite.' Shalmaneser claims that he 'slew 14,000 of their soldiers'. This battle is not mentioned in the Bible.

To date, this is the earliest reference to an Israelite king of the divided monarchy outside the Bible.

On the reverse side of this stela (that's Shalmaneser on the front) the Assyrian king names 'Ahab, the Israelite' as one of an alliance of kings he fought and defeated.

After Ahab came Jehu, a ruthless royal assassin who massacred Ahab's entire family (2 Kings 9–10). Jehu made a lot of enemies and needed a strong friend. Who better to get 'on side' but the powerful Shalmaneser III? Therefore Jehu hurried along with a few presents for Shalmaneser.

This black limestone obelisk pictures the kings of the nations bringing tribute to Shalmaneser. The inscription above the second row down tells us that 'Jehu of the house of Omri' brought tribute, and the rest of the line provides the inventory. The kneeling figure is most likely Jehu himself. If so, this is the only contemporary carving of an Israelite king that we have at present.

These are just two examples of how inscriptions confirm the existence of kings in the Bible.

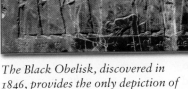

The Black Obelisk, discovered in 1846, provides the only depiction of an Israelite king found to date.

6. Sargon — the king who never lived?

The only reference to an Assyrian king called Sargon was found in just one verse in the Bible—Isaiah 20:1. Therefore it was assumed by some that he never really existed.

In 1843, a French archaeologist, Paul-Emil Botta, discovered the great city of Dur-Sharrukin ('Sargon's Fortress') at present day Khorsabad on the banks of the River Tigris to the northeast of Nineveh in modern Iraq. Sargon is now one of the best known Assyrian kings and was one of the most powerful rulers in the ancient world.

Sargon was a successful military commander and ruler. The uncovered city at Khorsabad revealed thousands of clay documents. His palace, with two hundred and forty rooms, was guarded by huge human-headed winged bulls each weighing around ten tons and standing 4.8m (15ft) high. The walls were lined with great slabs of stone carved with pictures and cuneiform writing.

One of the pair of human-headed winged bulls guarding the palace of Sargon.

Sargon had little time to enjoy his brand new city because he was killed in battle soon after. His son Sennacherib became king. Sennacherib is probably the man facing the king in this carving.

No one doubts the existence of Sargon today.

The figure on the left on this stone carving is king Sargon of Assyria.

7. A battle royal

One short verse in the Bible can reveal a long invasion: 'Sennacherib king of Assyria and all his forces were laying siege to Lachish' (1 Chronicles 32:9). No one can doubt that, because Sennacherib told the story in vivid detail.

When Sargon's son, Sennacherib, came to power in Assyria, he set out to plunder the land of Judah and capture Hezekiah, the king in Jerusalem. In the Bible, this invasion in 701 BC is graphically told in 2 Kings 18, 2 Chronicles 32 and Isaiah 36–37.

This is how Sennacherib described his campaign:

'As to Hezekiah, the Jew, he did not submit to my yoke, I laid siege to forty-six of his strong cities, walled forts and to the countless small villages in their vicinity, and conquered them by means of well-stamped earth ramps, and battering-rams brought near to the walls combined with the attack by foot soldiers, using mines, breeches as well as sapper work.'

But Sennacherib left an even more vivid description in stone.

In 1847 the British archaeologist, Austin Henry Layard, discovered the ruins of the Assyrian capital Nineveh, close to the modern town of Mosul. In the royal palace, a 'victory' room described the battle for Lachish in carved stone. This made international news because it was described in the Bible and was now dug out of the ground. Lachish was the second most important town in Judah next to Jerusalem.

Among the Assyrian army are the stone slingers—the artillery of the ancient world. Judges 20:16 is the oldest known reference to the sling; the tribe of Benjamin could boast 700 left-handed slingers who could aim at a hair and not miss!

Part of a 20 metre (65 ft) stone carving describing the siege of Lachish in 701 BC. Look for the battering rams, the defenders on the city towers, the assault troops scaling the walls, the people trying to escape the city, and prisoners impaled on stakes.

The Assyrian stone slingers at the siege of Lachish with a pile of shot at their feet.

These Assyrian stones from the battle in 701 BC were the size of a billiard ball and could reach a velocity in excess of 97 km/h (60 mph) over a distance of a quarter of a mile. Have you heard of David and the nine foot giant of Gath recorded in 1 Samuel 17:34–51?

8. Digging for victory!

Today, in Jerusalem you can walk through history—the very tunnel cut by Hezekiah's engineers to ensure a safe supply of water against an Assyrian siege.

Hezekiah had time to prepare for a long siege. To ensure that Jerusalem would have an adequate water supply and at the same time deny the Assyrians access to water, the Bible tells us that 'a large force' of Hezekiah's engineers diverted the water from 'the springs and the stream that flowed through the land' and 'channelled the water down to the west of the City of David' (2 Chronicles 32:4,30). This was achieved by a tunnel that ended in a pool safe within the city (2 Kings 20:20).

The tunnel excavated deep under the city of Jerusalem by Hezekiah's engineers by 701 BC.

This incredible piece of engineering was discovered in 1838. The underground channel was cut into the limestone rock and ran for 533 m (1748 ft) from the Gihon Spring near the floor of the Kidron Valley outside the eastern wall of the city and wound underground to a pool, safely within the city. At its deepest point the tunnel is almost 49 m (160 ft) below the surface.

We know that the engineers, working with small oil lamps and metal picks, began at both ends because they left a plaque in the wall at the point where they met in the middle.

No one can be sure how they achieved this. But no one doubts that the tunnel is the one referred to in the Bible.

In June 2004 workmen uncovered stone steps that led down to a large pool in Jerusalem. It is generally agreed by archaeologists that this is where Hezekiah's tunnel ended and is the 'Pool of Siloam' referred to in John 9:7,11.

The pool of Siloam received water though Hezekiah's underground aqueduct from the Gihon spring.

9. 'Like a bird in a cage'

In his own records of his military campaigns, there is only one king that Sennacherib admits that he did not capture—Hezekiah, the king of Judah. That is exactly what we find in the biblical account.

The prophet Isaiah had promised that no siege ramp would be set against Jerusalem (Isaiah 37:33-34), and archaeologists have found no evidence of a siege ramp against Jerusalem at this time. In fact, Sennacherib suddenly broke off his blockade of Jerusalem and hurried back to Assyria.

In 2 Kings 19:32–36 the Bible describes what happened. Unless the biblical record is true, why

On the Taylor Prism, discovered in the ruins of Nineveh in 1830, Sennacherib records his military exploits and how he shut up Hezekiah in Jerusalem 'like a bird in a cage'.

did Sennacherib return home without attempting to break into the capital? Babylonian and Greek records agree that a 'great multitude' of Assyrians died, forcing Sennacherib to end his campaign.

Back home in Nineveh, Sennacherib had to put the best spin on his defeat. The first was that 'victory room' in his palace recording the defeat of Lachish (see page 17). But on a clay prism recounting his campaigns he records the plunder he took from the land of Israel: 'I drove out of them 200,150 people, young and old, male and female, horses, mules, donkeys, camels, big and small cattle beyond counting, and considered them booty.' Then he adds: 'As to Hezekiah himself I made a prisoner in Jerusalem, his royal residence, like a bird in a cage.'

That last phrase was an unintended admission of failure!

The Bible claims that when Sennacherib returned home, he was later assassinated by two of his sons (2 Kings 19:37). Assyrian and Babylonian records confirm his assassination, though only the Bible provides the names of the assassins.

A Babylonian Chronicle for the year 681 BC reads, 'On the 20th day of the month Tibetu, Sennacherib, king of Assyria, his son killed him in a rebellion.'

10. 16 March 597 BC—precisely!

In a decisive battle at the Egyptian stronghold of Carchemish in 605 BC, the crown prince Nebuchadnezzar of Babylon took command of the army and fought with the Egyptians. The Egyptian army was soundly defeated.

The biblical prophet Jeremiah refers to this battle: 'This is the message against the army of Pharaoh Neco king of Egypt, which was defeated at Carchemish on the Euphrates River by Nebuchadnezzar king of Babylon…' (Jeremiah 46:2).

When Nebuchadnezzar became king in Babylon, Jehoiakim of Judah sent tribute to him as a subject king. But one day Jehoiakim withdrew his loyalty (2 Kings 24:1). The Babylonian army attacked Jerusalem, Jehoiakim was captured, and his son, Jehoiachin, was put on the throne. After three months, the Babylonians returned and 'Nebuchadnezzar took Jehoiachin captive to Babylon' (2 Kings 24:15).

Discovered in Babylon, this is part of the food ration for Jehoiachin 'king of the land of Judah' and his five sons when they were taken into exile in Babylon. This clay tablet is in the Museum in Berlin.

That phrase is confirmed by part of the food ration for king Jehoiachin of Judah and his family when they were exiled to Babylon by Nebuchadnezzar in 597 BC.

A small clay tablet, known as a Babylonian Chronicle, also records the defeat of Jerusalem at this time. It states that Nebuchadnezzar 'encamped against the city of Judah and on the second day of the month of Adar he seized the city and captured the king. He appointed there a king of his own choice, received its heavy tribute and sent them to Babylon.'

On this side of the Babylonian Chronicle the capture of Jerusalem on 16 March 597 BC is recorded. On the reverse side is the battle at Carchemish referred to in Jeremiah 46.

The exact day and month is recorded, and since their calendar followed the phases of the moon, scientists can date precisely the capture of Jerusalem by Nebuchadnezzar recorded in 2 Kings 24:10–17 as 16 March 597 BC.

11. Old Nabonidus had a son

Nabonidus was the last king of Babylon and the book of Daniel in the Bible says he had a son called Belshazzar. Not everyone agreed because this was the only knowledge we had of him.

In fact, the book of Daniel claims that Belshazzar was the king in Babylon when Daniel interpreted the message written on the wall by God during the king's riotous feast (Daniel 5). However, it was known that Nabonidus was the last king of Babylon when the Persians broke into the city in 539 BC. There was no reference outside the Bible to a king called Belshazzar. Therefore some assumed that the Bible was wrong.

In 1854 the British Consul in Basra discovered four identical time capsules at the corners of a temple

The clay Nabonidus Cylinder on which the king offers a prayer for himself and his son, Belshazzar.

Nabonidus had repaired. In these, the king offered a prayer for himself and 'Belshazzar my firstborn son, the offspring of my heart.' Since then, more inscriptions have been discovered referring to Belshazzar as 'the crown prince'.

It is now known that Nabonidus was away with his army in Arabia for around ten years and he put his son Belshazzar on the throne as co-regent. Clearly Belshazzar was enjoying himself at the feast when God sent him a warning just before the Persians broke into the city.

This also makes sense of a comment in Daniel 5:29 that as a reward for interpreting the 'writing on the wall' Daniel was made 'the third highest ruler in the kingdom.' Nabonidus was number one, Belshazzar was number two and Daniel could only be number three.

Like the Hittites, David and Sargon—all doubted by the critics at one time—no one can dispute the accuracy of the Bible when it refers to Belshazzar.

A stone relief of the Babylonian king, Nabonidus, worshipping three of his gods.

12. The order that was never given?

Three times the Bible claims that when the Persians came to power their king allowed the Jews to return from exile and rebuild their temple and city in Jerusalem. But critics said, 'Nonsense'.

I n 539 BC, during that feast of Belshazzar, the Persian army broke into the city of Babylon and became masters of a vast and fabulously wealthy empire. In the Bible, 2 Chronicles 36:23, Ezra 1:2–4 and Ezra 6:2–5 record that the Persian king, Cyrus, allowed the Jews to return home

and rebuild their temple and city. At one time critics said this was very unlikely because ancient kings took people away from their land and never sent them back.

In 1879 a clay cylinder, just 23 cms (9 inches) long, was discovered in the ruins of ancient Babylon. It is known as the Cyrus Cylinder and the inscription included an order allowing many nations to return from their exile, rebuild their cities and temple and take their gods with them; Persia would even pay some of the cost!

Part of the inscription reads: 'I returned them unharmed to their cells, in the sanctuaries that make them happy. May all the gods that I returned to their sanctuaries... ask for a long life for me, and mention my good deeds...'

There is no reference to the Jews on the Cylinder, but it confirms the enlightened policy of Cyrus and therefore the accuracy of those three passages in the Bible.

The Cyrus Cylinder is seen as possibly the earliest known charter of human rights. For this reason, it is a national icon of Iran, and a replica is in the United Nations Headquarters in New York. It has been translated into all the official languages of the UN.

13. 'A census of the entire Roman world'?

According to Luke 2:1–3, at the time of the birth of Jesus Christ, Caesar Augustus ordered every man to return to his 'own town' for the purpose of a census. Once again, critics claimed that was a very unlikely order.

The fact of a census in the time of Augustus is no longer in serious doubt. It has long been established that there were regular censuses in the Roman empire and that everyone was required to return to their home district for this purpose.

Discovered in Egypt in 1905, this papyrus comes from Egypt in AD 104 and in part reads '...it is essential that all those who are away from their homes be summoned to return to their own hearths...'.

A papyrus document discovered in Egypt reveals that in AD 104, the Roman Prefect (Governor) of Egypt, Gaius Vibius Maximus, ordered all those in his area who were away from their place of origin to return for the purpose of a census. They were ordered to go back to their 'home' in their original 'administrative district'.

Caesar Augustus came to power in 31 BC after the battle of Actium when he defeated Anthony and Cleopatra. He was the emperor at the time of the birth of Jesus.

But there was another problem in the claim, 'This was the first census while Quirinius was governor of Syria' (Luke 2:2). In fact, Sentius Saturninus was governor of Syria at the time of the census in 4 BC when Jesus was born, so how could the Bible claim it was Quirinius?

In answer to this, a renowned archaeologist, Sir William Ramsay, discovered that whilst Sentius Saturninus was governor of Syria at the time of the census in 4 BC,[*] Quirinius controlled the armies and directed the foreign policy of Syria. There are other examples of this across the empire. Quirinius was the senior of the two men.

---

[*] In case you are wondering, Jesus was born between 6 and 4 BC because of an error made in the 6th century AD in calculating the calendar.

14. Pontius Pilate was governor of Judea

In his Gospel, Luke refers to the time when John the Baptist began to preach. Every one of the seven people he mentions is known to history. Luke made no mistake.

'In the fifteenth year of the reign of Tiberius Caesar—when Pontius Pilate was governor of Judea, Herod tetrarch of Galilee, his brother Philip tetrarch of Iturea and Traconitis, and Lysanias tetrarch of Abilene—during the high priesthood of Annas and Caiaphas…' (Luke 3:1).

Pontius Pilate was the Roman Governor of Jerusalem who allowed the death of Jesus Christ. His military HQ was at Caesarea. A small stone plaque was discovered

there commemorating the fact that Pilate had dedicated a building to the emperor Tiberius. Though incomplete and broken, the inscription has been deciphered to read 'the Tiberium which Pontius Pilate, the Prefect of Judea dedicated'.

To date this is the only inscription with the name of Pilate, although his name appears in many contemporary texts.

This inscription, referring to Pontius Pilate and confirming his governorship of Judea, was discovered in 1961 at Caesarea.

Strangely, there are still some people who question whether Jesus really lived! However, here are a few of many witnesses outside the Bible who confirm the life of Jesus.

Tacitus is regarded as an accurate Roman historian in the first century. He referred to Christians and added, 'The founder of this name, Christus, had been executed in the reign of Tiberius by the procurator Pontius Pilate.'

Josephus was a Jew born four years after the crucifixion of Jesus and he refers to the stoning of James as 'the brother of Jesus, who was called Christ [Messiah], whose name was James'. Historians have found no reason to doubt the genuineness of this text.

Celsus, a second century Roman philosopher strongly opposed to the Christian faith, never once argued against the reality of Jesus.

Lucian of Samosata was a second century Greek satirist who ridiculed the Christians and Christ but never suggested that he did not live.

There is not a single text in Jewish or pagan literature in the first few centuries that ever denies the historical reality of Jesus.

A small bronze coin from the time of Pilate bears the emblem of a staff and the name of Tiberius Caesar. It was minted in Jerusalem in the seventeenth year of Tiberius c. AD 31—close to the year of the death of Jesus.

15. Luke, an accurate historian

Paul was accompanied on many of his journeys by Luke, a physician by profession. Luke wrote the Gospel of Luke and the Acts of the Apostles. He was an accurate historian.

In his Gospel and Acts, Luke names 117 separate living people, 114 towns, provinces, islands, seas and other identifiable places, and 25 political, military, social or religious events known to history.

Luke's order of events and location of towns and provinces, his knowledge of Roman administration, censuses and regiments, his naming of national and local officials and of Jewish rituals, law and festivals, are all faultless.

Sir William Ramsay, a scholar honoured by British, Continental and American universities and knighted for his service to archaeology, concluded after a lifetime of research: 'You may press the words of Luke in a degree beyond any other historian's and they stand the keenest scrutiny and the hardest treatment.' He added: 'Christianity did not originate in a lie and we can and must demonstrate this.'

Luke must have kept a journal. And why not?

We know that books were widely read in the first century. Every Jewish male was expected to be able to read and it was common for civil servants and others to use 'notebooks' for their work. Matthew, Zacchaeus, the centurion, and the estate workers in the parable of Luke 16:6 were each able to read and write. The Ethiopian was reading his personal copy of the prophet Isaiah when Philip met with him (Acts 8:28).

Across Judea, marriage and divorce documents, food lists, orders for merchandise, soldiers' pay slips, legal documents and graffiti have been found. Often texts were in more than one language. The text above the cross was written in Aramaic, Latin and Greek (John 19:19–20). Most people in Judea were at least bilingual (Aramaic and Greek) and Jesus preached in both.

In 2 Timothy 4:13, Paul asked Timothy to bring with him 'my scrolls, especially the parchments'. The word for 'parchments' referred to an early form of notebook made of parchment or slivers of wood—rather like a ring binder!

The idea that the New Testament Gospels were not written until well into the second century must now be abandoned.

The Greeks had no word to describe this first century notebook so they borrowed the Latin word membranae.

16. Intelligent men

Of the many names Luke mentions in the Acts of the Apostles that fit perfectly with known history, here are just three.

The ruins of the Theatre for which Erastus laid the pavement.

On their first missionary journey, Paul and Barnabas stopped off at Paphos in Cyprus and they came into contact with the Roman proconsul **Sergius Paulus**. Luke describes him as 'an intelligent man' and that he 'believed, for he was amazed at the teaching of the Lord' (Acts 13:7,12).

In 1877, an inscription was found near Paphos, bearing the name of (Sergius) Paulus and his title of proconsul. It is dated to AD 47 when Paul and Barnabas were on the island. Another inscription found in Rome confirms this.

When Paul was in Corinth, he wrote to the church at Rome and included greetings from **Erastus**, whom he called 'the city's director of public works' (Romans 16:23). The word Paul uses refers to one who is in charge of public finances. Outside the ruins of the theatre at Corinth is an inscription on a marble paving slab that reads, 'Erastus, in return for his aedileship, laid this pavement at his own expense.' The aedile was, among other duties, in charge of city finance.

The inscription from Paphos bearing the name of the Proconsul Sergius Paulus who is named in Acts 13.

Erastus was an uncommon name at this time. Erastus, the city official who paid for the pavement outside the theatre in Corinth, became a Christian and sent greetings to the church at Rome.

While Paul was in Corinth, he was brought to trial before **Gallio** whom Luke describes as 'proconsul of Achaia' (Acts 18:12) The accuracy of this is confirmed by an inscription that confirms Gallio was proconsul of Achaia in AD 52.

This Latin inscription, discovered in Corinth in 1929, informs us that Erastus laid the pavement outside the theatre at his own expense.

These three officials are examples of many names in the Acts of the Apostles that are known to history. Again, Luke is seen to be a careful and accurate historian.

Part of the 'Gallio Inscription', discovered at Delphi in Greece in 1905. In the fourth line from the top (highlighted here) the Greek word for 'Gallio' is clearly visible.

17. The unknown God at Athens

In Athens, Paul found himself in a very religious city. Idols and temples were everywhere. But someone was missing.

Below the Parthenon in Athens is a bare marble hill that, long before Paul's arrival in AD 50, had been the site of criminal trials. Its name, the Areopagus, referred to Ares the Greek god of war—although the Romans knew him as Mars. Here on Mars Hill, Paul debated with some of the many philosophers who, according to Luke, 'spent their time doing nothing but talking about and listening to the latest ideas' (Acts 17:21).

Walking around the city, Paul had found an altar with an inscription: 'To an unknown god' (Acts 17:23). Apparently 500 years earlier a plague led the people of Athens to believe that some unknown god must be angry, so an altar was set up to it and the plague stopped. Paul thought it would be a good way to introduce the only true God to them:

'The God who made the world and everything in it is the Lord of heaven and earth and does not live in temples built by hands. And he is not served by human hands, as if he needed anything, because he himself gives all men life and breath and everything else. From one man he made every nation of men, that they should inhabit the whole earth; and he determined the times set for them and the exact places where they should live… Therefore, since we are God's offspring, we should not think that the divine being is like gold or silver or stone—an image made by man's design and skill. In the past God overlooked such ignorance, but now he commands all people everywhere to repent. For he has set a day when he will judge the world with justice by the man he has appointed. He has given proof of this to all men by raising him from the dead' (Acts 17:24–31).

Paul's conclusion that the Creator has set a day for everyone to be held to account and that the proof of this is the resurrection of Jesus Christ, was sure to bring a response—some 'sneered', other showed interest, but a few 'believed' (Acts 17:32–34).

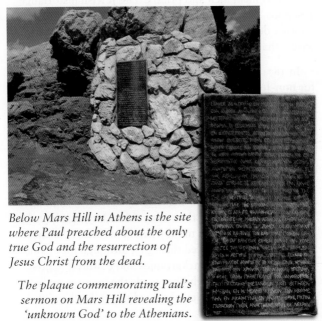

Below Mars Hill in Athens is the site where Paul preached about the only true God and the resurrection of Jesus Christ from the dead.

The plaque commemorating Paul's sermon on Mars Hill revealing the 'unknown God' to the Athenians.

18. A city divided

Although both Jew and non-Jew could walk quite freely around the city of Jerusalem, there was one place the non-Jew did not dare to tread.

The newly completed temple built by Herod the Great in Jerusalem was surrounded by an open courtyard with covered porticos. This was the 'court of the Gentiles (the non-Jews)'. Beyond this were courts only for the Jewish women, men and priests. The Jewish historian, Josephus, describes pillars at equal distance from one another declaring, some in Greek and some in Roman letters that 'no foreigner should go within that sanctuary.'

In 1871 a notice carved in stone and written in Greek for non-Jews was discovered in Jerusalem. It was dated to the first century and the letters were originally painted in red—remnants of the colour still remain. It read:

> 'No foreigner may pass the barrier and enclosure surrounding the temple. Anyone who is caught doing so will be himself to blame for his resulting death.'

Paul knew that it was the tragedy of many religions to separate people rather than unite them. He must have had this very inscription in mind when he wrote to the church at Ephesus and reminded them that although they came from many different backgrounds and cultures: 'Christ himself is our peace, who has made the two one and has destroyed the barrier, the dividing wall of hostility' (Ephesians 2:14).

Jesus himself taught his disciples to love their enemies (Matthew 5:44) and prayed that his followers 'may be brought to complete unity' (John 17:23).

Referring to his imminent death on a cross Jesus promised, 'When I am lifted up from the earth, I will draw all men to myself' (John 12:32). He meant all kinds of people from all kinds of backgrounds.

The Christian message invites all people—whatever their culture, language or background—to become united by trusting in Jesus.

The warning against any Gentile passing beyond the 'court of the Gentiles'.

19. Crucifixion?

From inscriptions we know that crucifixion, in one form or another, was common across the ancient world for prisoners of war, criminals and slaves.

The Persians crucified 3,000 Babylonians on one occasion, Alexander the Great crucified 2,000 after the siege of Tyre, and in 71 BC 6,000 rebels captured in the final defeat of Spartacus were crucified along the Via Appia from Rome to Capua. The Roman General Titus crucified 500 in one night during the siege of Jerusalem in AD 70.

But there was no archaeological evidence for any crucifixion—no skeletons of crucified men.

Then, in 1968 a 'bone box' was discovered in Jerusalem containing the bones of a young child and a young man. The inscription on the box states that the man, Yehohanan (John), had been 'hanged with knees apart'—that meant he was crucified. The right heel bone of the

This ankle bone of a crucified man in the time of Pilate provides cruel evidence of crucifixion. But it is the only archaeological evidence of the practice.

man had a Roman iron nail driven through it. The end of the nail had buckled, making it impossible to remove when the bones were later gathered into the box.

It is beyond doubt that Jesus Christ was crucified as described in the Bible. Paul reminded the church at Corinth: 'I resolved to know nothing while I was with you except Jesus Christ and him crucified' (1 Corinthians 2:2). But why was that so important?

Again, it is Paul who gives us the answer simply: 'Christ died for our sins' (1 Corinthians 15:3). It was so that he could take our rebellion against God and the punishment it deserved by God, on himself. 'He became sin for us' (2 Corinthians 5:21) so that we could be forgiven and go free.

In the early centuries, Christians were mocked for their belief in a Saviour who was crucified, but it did not stop them from trusting in him.

This second century graffiti in Rome shows a donkey-headed man and the mocking inscription that 'Alexamenos worships his god'. Someone has written underneath 'Alexamenos is faithful.' Perhaps Alexamenos himself added that!

20. He is not here — he has risen!

Everywhere in the New Testament, the resurrection of Jesus Christ is assumed as a historical fact.

Paul concluded: 'Christ died for our sins according to the Scriptures, he was buried, he was raised on the third day according to the Scriptures' (1 Corinthians 15:3–4).

Obviously we cannot expect archaeological evidence for the resurrection! However, everything about the account of his death and resurrection agrees with what we know of first century practices. For example, to request the body from Pilate was something allowed by Roman law, and it was the custom to anoint a body with spices and then wrap it in strips of linen (John 19:38-40).

The Christians' last prayer—*A vivid portrayal of what we know happened to Christians in the first two hundred years. Christians were torn apart for the entertainment of the crowds, and other were burned to death on stakes. But the more Christians were killed, the more the church grew in numbers.*

At first, Christianity was not seen as a great threat to the pagan religions of Rome, but soon things changed. The Roman historian, Tacitus, described the terrible suffering of Christians under the emperor Nero in the first century: how he poured pitch over the Christians and set light to them to illuminate his garden parties. Other were sent to the arena to be mauled by wild animals.

Why were they prepared to die so horribly? Because they firmly believed in the resurrection of Jesus Christ, that he was alive and with them in their suffering.

Diogneto, a pagan writing in the middle of the second century, admitted that the Christians 'thrown to the wild beasts do not allow themselves to be beaten,' and he added, 'The more they are punished, the more the others increase in numbers.'

Tertullian, a church leader at the same time, commented on the cruel martyrdom of Christians: 'The blood is the seed of Christians.' He meant, the witness of martyred Christians leads many others to become Christians.

People knew their faith must be real and wanted to know the risen Christ for themselves.

Nothing has changed two thousand years later.

The Garden Tomb in Jerusalem is similar to the tomb in which Jesus' body would have been laid.

Before you go...

We began this little book with the comment that too often people dismiss the Bible as unreliable without realising that archaeologists have uncovered so many things that confirm its accuracy.

We have now seen just a few of the many discoveries that show the Bible to be reliable. The full book advertised on the opposite page provides many more.

Of course, we do not have sufficient information to prove every statement in the Bible, but if we can trust it wherever we can check it, then we have good reason to trust it everywhere as a reliable record of what God wants us to know about the origin of the universe, the human race, and his great plan of salvation.

The Christian Bible is without doubt the most influential book the world has ever known. This is because from the beginning to the end it is pointing towards Jesus Christ who came into this world not only to set us a perfect example of a life without sin, but more significantly to give his life on the cross to take the guilt, sin and punishment in place of all who will put their trust in him. This way we can have peace with God.

Jesus rose again from the dead to keep his promise to be with all those who trust in him — whoever and wherever they are.

The apostle Paul wrote to the church at Corinth:

'Christ died for our sins according to the Scriptures, He was buried, and He was raised on the third day according to the Scriptures.'

1 Corinthians 15, verses 3–4